SUPERSTITIONS SURROUNDING

CROSSING YOUR FINGERS

Sharon Dalgleish

Stride
An Imprint of The Child's World®
childsworld.com

Published by The Child's World®
800-599-READ • childsworld.com

Copyright © 2023 by The Child's World®
All rights reserved. No part of this book may be reproduced or utilized in any form or by any means without written permission from the publisher.

Photography Credits
Photographs ©: Laugesen Mateo/Shutterstock Images, cover, 1; Teerapong Kunkaeo/Shutterstock Images, 5; Kraken Images/Shutterstock Images, 6, 17; Juergen Hu/Shutterstock Images, 9; Viacheslav Lopatin/Shutterstock Images, 11; Jan Kangurowski/iStockphoto, 12; Shutterstock Images, 15, 19; Blue Cutler/iStockphoto, 20; Dean Drobot/Shutterstock Images, 21

ISBN Information
9781503865129 (Reinforced Library Binding)
9781503866423 (Portable Document Format)
9781503867260 (Online Multi-user eBook)
9781503868106 (Electronic Publication)

LCCN 2022939697

Printed in the United States of America

About the Author
Sharon Dalgleish lives in Sydney, Australia. She never opens an umbrella inside or walks under a ladder. But she does have a black cat.

CONTENTS

CHAPTER ONE
Fingers Crossed . . . 4

CHAPTER TWO
Crossing Centuries and Cultures . . . 10

CHAPTER THREE
Does It Work? . . . 16

Glossary . . . 22
Fast Facts . . . 23
One Stride Further . . . 23
Find Out More . . . 24
Index . . . 24

FINGERS CROSSED

There is a **superstition** surrounding finger crossing. Some people think the **gesture** will bring them good luck. They think it might make their wishes come true. People do not have to keep all that luck to themselves. They can cross their fingers to wish someone else luck, too.

> One part of the superstition says that if a person crosses his or her fingers while moving through a graveyard, it will scare off the **Devil**.

In ancient times, some people would cross their finger with another person. They believed their wishes would be protected at the point where their fingers met.

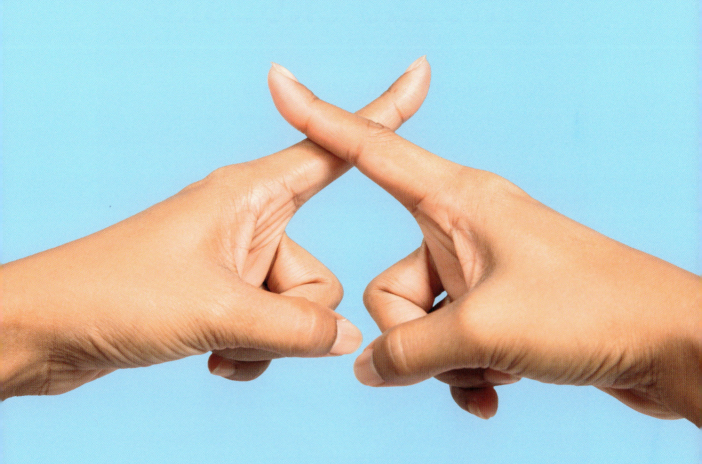

People cross their fingers in many different situations. Sometimes people do this when wishing for their favorite team to win.

To do this, people can place their middle finger across their pointer finger. This forms what is called a St. Andrew's cross. It is the most common way for a person to cross his or her fingers. A person may cross his or her fingers to get good luck. But it is also a way to avoid bad luck. For example, people sometimes cross their fingers when making a promise. They believe this gesture will protect them from any bad luck that comes if they break the promise.

A person may also use this gesture when telling a lie. If someone crosses his or her fingers while lying, the cross cancels out any bad luck he or she might get from telling a lie. But the crossed fingers should be hidden. If another person sees the crossed fingers and pulls them apart, there is no protection. Then the person has to tell the truth!

Before crossing fingers, some people tuck their thumb inside of their fist. This hand gesture is thought to protect people from evil. Today, this gesture is used in Scandinavia, the Netherlands, and Germany.

Crossing fingers was originally a prayer for God's protection or forgiveness. Today, some people still cross their fingers when making a promise so they won't be punished if they break it.

CHAPTER TWO

CROSSING CENTURIES AND CULTURES

The cross is a Christian **symbol**. Some Christians lived in the Roman **Empire**. This empire existed thousands of years ago. It spanned across Europe and into the Middle East and North Africa. Christians often had to hide their religion from Roman officials. So, they made a secret handshake. That way, they could recognize each other. It involved two people crossing fingers. Each person held out a thumb and pointer finger in an *L* shape. Then the two people touched thumbs and crossed pointer fingers.

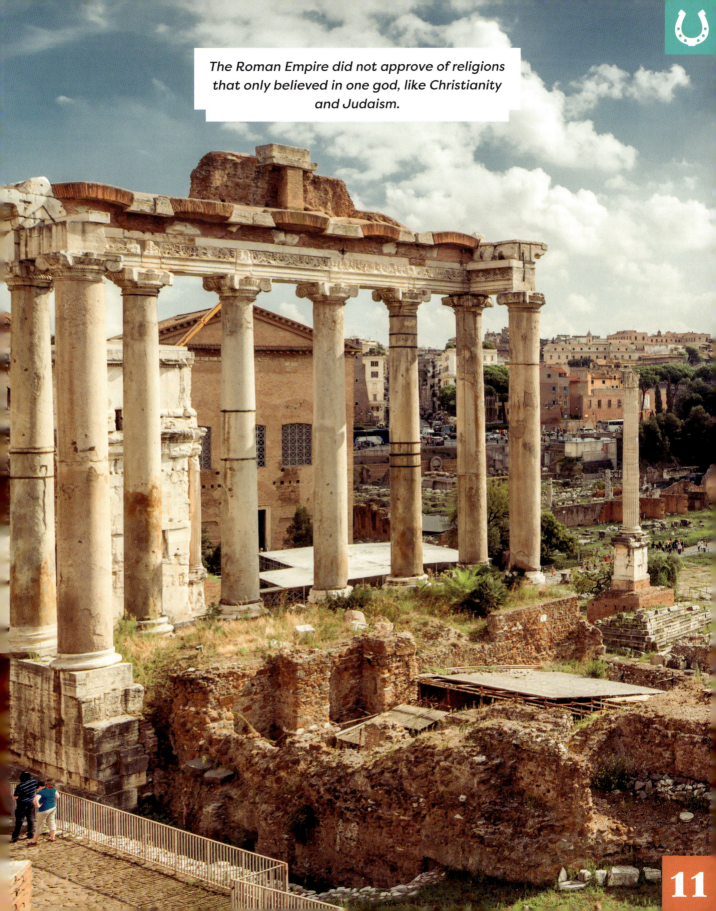

The Roman Empire did not approve of religions that only believed in one god, like Christianity and Judaism.

The secret handshake used by Christians made a symbol called the Ichthys, sometimes known as the Jesus fish.

Crossing fingers behind one's back might have started during this time, too. Roman officials wanted Christians to reject their religion. Some Christians were frightened. They denied their beliefs. When they did, they crossed their fingers behind their backs. No one knows for sure why. It might have been for luck so that the Romans would believe the lie. Or it might have been to ask God to forgive the lie.

In England during the Middle Ages (500–1500 AD), people carved symbols around doorways, windows, and fireplaces. These symbols were called witch marks. Many of the marks were crosses. Some people thought the symbols would keep evil from entering a house. Others thought the symbols would bring good luck.

The modern way of crossing fingers may have started around this time. Soldiers were fighting in the Hundred Years' War (1337–1453). This was a conflict between France and England. The soldiers needed luck. But it was not easy to cross fingers with another person in the middle of a battle. So, some soldiers crossed their own fingers instead.

The cross is a symbol used all over the world. Crosses can look different from each other. They are even sometimes disguised as something else. For example, a cross could be a flower with four petals. In Norse mythology, the thunder god Thor has a cross-shaped hammer. Some people believe his hammer is equal to the Christian cross's meaning and power. The basic meaning of the cross symbol stays the same. It is a symbol of protection.

> In the 1500s in England, people crossed their fingers to protect themselves from other people's sneezes. Sneezes were sometimes the sign of a serious illness.

Some people hang crosses in their houses or wear cross necklaces for protection.

Crossing fingers is common across many cultures, too. People do it in the United States, the United Kingdom, Spain, and France. In each of these places, the cross is a protective charm. It is used to prevent bad luck or to bring good luck.

Crossing fingers is a rude gesture in Vietnam. It is worse than using the middle finger in the United States.

CHAPTER THREE

DOES IT WORK?

People crossed their fingers in ancient times. Some people still do this today. This shows that superstitions pass from **generation** to generation. Modern science reminds people that superstitions are not true. There is no proof that crossing fingers will bring people good luck. People also do not get bad luck from not crossing their fingers. However, even when people know superstitions are not true, they sometimes do certain actions (like crossing fingers) anyway. That is because doing the action sometimes makes people feel better.

Today, some people believe that saying "fingers crossed" is enough to give or get good luck.

It can feel better to do something rather than nothing. Johnny Oates was a Texas Rangers baseball manager. He once sat in the dugout with his arms and ankles crossed. He told everyone he was not superstitious. Then he crossed his eyes. Oates knew the superstition was not true. But he crossed everything anyway.

The way people cross their fingers is still **evolving**. Today, some people use technology to send a fingers-crossed **emoji**.

Some people cross their legs for good luck.

Crossing fingers can make people feel more in control. A university studied what happened when people crossed their fingers before doing a task. They found that it made people feel more confident. People's performance improved.

Another study looked at pain. People with pain in their pointer finger were told to cross their fingers. The pain was reduced a bit. The crossed fingers confused the way the brain processed pain signals. So, some people think crossed fingers might reduce pain.

Around the 500s in England, some people tied string to one of their fingers. They thought the knot would tie them to good luck.

Crossing fingers can be a source of comfort for people, but it should not be used in place of hard work.

However, relying on crossed fingers for luck can mean people may not prepare properly for a task. For example, if a person does not study for a test, crossing his or her fingers during the test will not help the person get a good grade. People still need to make their own luck, no matter how much they believe in a superstition.

GLOSSARY

Devil (DEV-uhl) The Devil is a powerful spirit of evil. Some people ward off the Devil by crossing their fingers.

emoji (eh-MOH-jee) An emoji is a small image used to show a feeling or an idea. Some people text the fingers-crossed emoji to friends to wish them luck.

empire (EM-pire) An empire is a group of people or land under one leader. Most people in the Roman Empire believed in multiple gods.

evolving (eh-VOLV-ing) Evolving means slowly changing over time. The way people feel about superstitions is evolving.

generation (jen-uh-RAY-shuhn) A group of people born around the same time is called a generation. A generation may pick up superstitious actions from an older generation.

gesture (JES-chur) A gesture is used to communicate a feeling or intention by moving part of the body. A person crossing his or her fingers is making a hand gesture.

superstition (soo-pur-STIH-shuhn) A superstition is a belief that certain events cause good or bad luck. It is a common superstition to cross your fingers for good luck.

symbol (SIM-buhl) A symbol is a design or object that stands for something else. A cross can be a symbol for protection.

FAST FACTS

- Crossing fingers is said to bring a person good luck or stop bad luck.

- Some people see the cross as a symbol of protection.

- People have crossed their fingers in different ways throughout history.

- Christians in the Roman Empire had a secret handshake to help them identify other Christians.

- Scientists have found that people may feel more confident after crossing their fingers.

ONE STRIDE FURTHER

- Talk to your friends or family. Ask them if they have crossed their fingers and why. Write down what you found out.

- Why do you think crossing fingers is a popular superstition today?

- Do you think people should stop crossing their fingers for luck? Explain your answer.

FIND OUT MORE

IN THE LIBRARY

Alexander, Heather. *A Child's Introduction to Norse Mythology.* New York, NY: Black Dog & Leventhal Publishers, 2018.

Ancient Rome. New York, NY: DK Publishing, 2020.

Sonneborn, Liz. *Sneezing.* Parker, CO: The Child's World, 2023.

ON THE WEB

Visit our website for links about crossing your fingers:
childsworld.com/links

Note to Parents, Teachers, and Librarians: We routinely verify our Web links to make sure they are safe and active sites. So encourage your readers to check them out!

INDEX

charm, 15
Christians, 10, 12
cross, 14–15, 18, 20

Devil, 4

emoji, 18
England, 13, 14

lie, 8, 12

promise, 7

Roman, 10, 12

science, 16
soldiers, 13
symbol, 10, 13, 14

Vietnam, 15